Want to know
*nature*

# All About Cats

## Jozua Douglas & Hiky Helmantel

Clavis
**NEW YORK**

Ah, there she is! Grandpa has brought her!
Grandpa is going on holiday and Stormy
can't go with him. "Cats don't like long journeys,"
Grandpa says. Jonas doesn't mind at all.
"I'll take good care of her, Grandpa," he promises.

# What are cats?

Cats have **teeth** so **sharp** they can tear flesh.

Cats use their **tails** to keep their balance when they climb trees. And a cat's tail tells you if he is angry, scared or sad.

Cats use their **whiskers** to see how close things are – that way they don't bump their heads.

Cats are cuddly animals. Usually they love people and love to snuggle up with their humans. Cats can live to be eighteen to twenty years old. That's very old in cat years. Old enough to be grandpas and grandmas.

Cats have **super sensitive hearing**. They hear sounds you don't even know about. Listen very carefully. Do you hear mice pattering about? Do you hear sparrows hopping? Bugs running? A cat can hear all of those sounds. And can you move your ears? Cats can turn their ears in all directions, so they know exactly where a sound is coming from.

Cats see the world very differently from humans. They don't **see** colors that well and they can't see the color red at all! But cats can see really well in the dark. Cats don't have to put on a light when they go to the litter box at night.

Cats have excellent **noses**. They smell things you can't. Maybe you think the cat's litter box isn't smelly, but a cat might disagree.

Did you know cats always land on their feet when they fall? They are flexible and turn right way up super fast. Cats have even survived falls from high apartment buildings.

# The cat family

Cats are sweet cuddly animals. But they are animals of prey too.
Did you know they are related to lions and tigers?
A cat is kind of like a mini tiger.

**Tigers** are the biggest cats of them all.
They hunt big animals like deer,
buffalos and boars.

Unfortunately
there are not many
tigers left. Some people
hunt them for their
beautiful soft coats
and then use them as rugs!

**Lions** are called
the king of beasts.
The male lion has a beautiful mane
and looks very fierce. Lions hunt
big animals like buffalos, buck,
and zebras.

**Cheetahs** are the fastest animal on earth.
They can run as fast as cars on a highway.
They hunt hares, young warthogs,
gazelles and antelopes.

**Leopards** have beautiful spotted fur. They usually hunt at night. They sneak up on their prey – animals like deer, antelopes, lizards, birds and monkeys – and jump on top of them.

**Wildcats** look a lot like house cats, but are bigger. They hunt small animals like mice, rats and rabbits.

**Lynx** live in the forest. They are bigger than cats, but smaller than lions. Lynx have tufts on their ears. They eat rabbits, hares, birds, deer, sheep and goats.

# What do cats say?

Do you want to know how to talk to cats? They speak a different language from the ones humans speak. Cats purr, growl, cry and meow. You should also pay attention to their tails, because their tails tell you a lot.

## I feel happy

Cats purr when they feel happy.
Purrs sound like soft grunts.
Purrs say: "I like being with you."

## I am angry

When cats are angry, they make themselves bigger. Their fur stands on end and they arch their backs. They sweep their tails back and forth and flatten their ears. If they spit or hiss they are saying: "Careful, I am angry. Stay away!"

## I'm afraid

When cats are scared, they make themselves very small. They hold their ears flat on their heads and their eyes get big. They keep their tails low. Be careful because a scared cat could attack you for no reason you can see.

## Meow

Cats meow when they want to tell you something. If they really want your attention they might even start to howl. Did you know cats meow in different ways? Listen carefully. When your cat wants to go outside, his meow will sound different from the way he meows when he wants food.

## You are mine

Cats love to rub their heads against you.
It makes you start to smell like them
and that's important to a cat. To you he's saying
"You are mine." And to other cats he's saying
"This one belongs to me!"

## This is my spot

Each cat has his own smell and wants everything to smell
like him. That's why he rubs the chair leg with his head, and
why he scratches the couch. Sometimes he even pees. Those
are the ways he leaves his scent and tells other cats:

"This is my spot."

## How are you?

Cats like to sniff at things. It's how they find out if
there are other cats around. Sniffing tells them
exactly who stopped by, when, and if the
other cat is a boy or a girl.

### Did you know
cats and dogs don't
understand each other at all?
When a dog wags his tail,
he is usually cheerful.
When a cat wags his tail,
he is upset.

How do you take care of cats?

**The litter box** is your cat's private toilet. You have to clean it every day and change the cat litter twice a week.

Cats can take excellent care of themselves. They don't really need you to take care of them! Cats don't need to take baths, they wash themselves by licking their fur. Cats love being brushed, but you need to be careful or else your cat will get mad. Long haired cats need to be brushed often, at least once a week.

Cats usually sleep in their own baskets. But sometimes they like to lie on a sofa, on a windowsill, or near a nice warm heater.

## What do cats eat?

Cats know exactly when it is dinner time. Sometimes they even come to get you. *Meow meow.* That means: "It is time for dinner! Go and get me some food, quick!"

Cats eat twice a day. You can give them dried pet food or canned pet food. They love meat, but sometimes they also eat grass. It's healthy for them, just like vegetables are healthy for you.

# What do cats like?

Cats like to sit on your lap where it's soft and warm.
Try stroking your cat under his chin. Cats love that.
He'll start to purr immediately!

Cats like to play, but only when they feel like it.
In that way they are different from dogs
who are always ready to play.

Cats like to sit by the window. They can sit
silently and stare outside for hours. The window
is like a big television screen to a cat.

Cats like hunting. They prowl through
the garden looking for mice and birds.
When a cat sees a mouse, he stalks it.
He moves very quietly, the tip of his tail
moves back and forth... then he jumps
on top of it.

Did you ever get a dead mouse as a gift?
When a cat gives you a dead mouse,
it means: "Let's go hunting. I'll teach you how."

## Did you know
cats are really lazy?
They sleep twice as much
as humans.

# Cat shows

At cat shows proud owners show their cats and compete to see who has the prettiest cat of all. Look at those beautiful cats!

# What do cats hate?

Cats don't like loud sounds. You should not interrupt them when they are eating or sitting in the litter box. Sometimes cats will accidentally catch a frog. But usually they avoid them because frogs can scream really loud when they are scared. And cats don't like that.

Cats don't like water either. And they really don't like rough games. Never pull a cat's tail. And don't touch their ears either. They find it very annoying.

The owners try their best
to make their cats look pretty.
They cut and comb
and blow-dry until
their cats look tip-top.

**5** Sneak through the grass quietly.

**6** Choose an animal that isn't too big.

**7** Pounce on your prey.

**8** Enjoy your meal!

**9** Or would you rather eat something else?

At cat shows there are also shops where you can buy all sorts of cat things, like baskets, leashes, brushes, bows and toys.

The prettiest cat wins a prize – and might even win a part in a cat commercial.

The judges look at every cat from all angles. Is the fur nice and shiny? Is the color right? Does the cat have spots? And are they in the right place? Is the tail long enough? Does the cat have pretty teeth, eyes and ears?

2

1

3

# Kittens

A baby cat is called a kitten. Sometimes a mother cat will give birth to as many as eight babies. They grow inside the mother's belly and are born after about two months. They are small, bald, wriggling little animals. They look like mice.

**Did you know** a kitten's eyes are always blue at first? The color usually changes later.

It's best not to take her kittens away from a mother cat. No matter how sweet she usually is, she might not like it and could get very angry.

After about a week they open their eyes. The kittens drink milk from their mother, so she needs to eat three to four times a day. If the mother cat doesn't have enough milk the kittens are fed milk from a bottle. After three months the little cats are big enough to go to a new home.

# The cat doctor

Cats have to go to the doctor once a year.
The vet checks to see if the cat is healthy
and gives the cat shots so she doesn't get sick.

If a cat scratches himself a lot, he might have fleas. Fleas are tiny little creatures that make a cat very itchy. The vet might give the cat a flea collar to help.

It's usually easy to tell if a cat is sick. A healthy cat
has clear eyes and a wet nose. He has clean teeth, ears, nose and eyes
and thick and shiny fur. If a cat doesn't feel like eating, he might be ill.

**The Egyptian Mau –** is a cat with beautifully spotted fur. The forelegs are a bit shorter than the hind legs.

**The Maine Coon –** has longish hair, a thick, full tail and tufts of hair on the tips of its ears.

**The Abyssinian –** might be the smartest cat of all. These cats are full of mischief and are big show-offs.

## How many types of cats are there?

There are more than one hundred types of cats. Cats can be short-haired or long-haired, have round ears or pointy ears, and eyes that are round or almond-shaped.

**The Persian –** is a quiet, calm cat with long hair and a very sweet temperament.

**The Russian Blue –** has soft fur and beautiful eyes. These cats don't like noise and love being inside.

**The Bengal** – looks like a tiger. Bengal cats are yellow or orange and have black stripes or spots.

**The Birman** – looks very sweet and is very sweet too.

**The Manx** – doesn't have a tail, or has a very short one. Manx cats love playing games and are very sweet to children.

**The Siamese** – is a people lover. These cats are smart and are quick learners. Siamese cats meow a lot – they are real talkers.

**The Selkirk Rex** – is a cat with long curly hair, a beautiful round head and round eyes.

**The Regular house cat** – is the cat you see most often. They exist in different colors: white, black, gray and red. Some have stripes or spots.

**The Sphynx** – is all bald and wrinkly. They need to take a bath once a week and are always hungry.

# I Love Little Kitty

I love little kitty,
Her coat is so warm,
And if I don't hurt her,
She'll do me no harm.

So I'll not pull her tail,
Nor drive her away,

But kitty and I
Together will play.

She will sit by my side,
And I'll give her some food,
And she'll like me because
I'm gentle and good.

-Traditional

# Fat Cat

A cat sits on the mat
and
dreams of cream
and
mice that taste nice.
It's no wonder
that
the cat is fat

# Make a cat picture frame!

**This is what you do:**

**This is what you need:**
- A piece of strong white paper or cardboard
- Scissors
- Colored pencils
- Glue
- An empty toilet roll
- A nice picture or photograph

1 Draw the shape of a cat on the paper and cut it out.

2 Put your picture on its belly and trace it. Now draw the paws and carefully cut around them, so you can put your picture behind the paws.

3 Decorate your cat frame.

4 Glue an empty toilet roll to the back, so your frame will stand up.

5 Your picture frame is done!

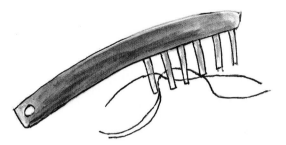